NoLex 1|13

PEACHTREE CITY LIBRARY
201 Willowbend Road
Peachtree, GA 30269

Artist of the Wild

JOHN JAMES AUDUBON

by Martha E. Kendall

A Gateway Green Biography
The Millbrook Press
Brookfield, Connecticut

Cover photo courtesy of The Bettman Archive
Background cover photo courtesy of Superstock

Photos courtesy of: American Museum of Natural
History: pp. 4, 8, 35, 40; Giraudon/Art Resource:
p. 12; The New-York Historical Society: pp. 15, 28,
37 (top); Library of Congress: pp. 18, 21, 31, 32;
Mill Grove Museum, Audubon, Pa.: p. 24 (both);
The Filson Club, Louisville, Ky.: p. 27; John James
Audubon State Park, Henderson, Ky.: p. 37 (bot-
tom); Museum of the City of New York: p. 39.

Library of Congress Cataloging-in-Publication Data

Kendall, Martha E, 1947–

John James Audubon : artist of the wild /
by Martha E. Kendall.
p.   cm. — (Gateway biography)
Includes bibliographical references and index.
Summary: Traces the life of John James Audubon
from his early childhood in France to his career
in America and his eventual success as an artist
and naturalist.
ISBN 1–56294–297–2
1. Audubon, John James, 1785–1851—Juvenile literature.
2. Ornithologists—United States—Biography—Juvenile
literature. 3. Animal painters—United States—Biography—Juvenile literature. [1. Audubon, John James,
1785–1851. 2. Artists. 3. Naturalists.]
QL31.A9K46   1993
598'.092—DC20
[B]   92–11423   CIP   AC

Published by The Millbrook Press
2 Old New Milford Road
Brookfield, Connecticut 06804

John James Audubon

John James Audubon, famous for his paintings of birds and animals, was one of America's first naturalists.

Young *John Audubon* was full of surprises. What could be in his pocket today? A toy boat? A fire engine? Marbles? Not likely. It was probably a sparrow's egg, carefully wrapped in soft cloth. Or maybe it was a frog, green and wet from its marshy home. Or it could have been a finch's nest, whose dry twigs poked out of John's bulging pocket. But no matter what treasure John found, his stepmother admired it.

John was no ordinary boy, and she was no ordinary stepmother. John was born on April 26, 1785, in Santo Domingo (now Haiti), in the Caribbean Sea. His father was a French sea captain who named his only son after himself—Jean Jacques (French for John James) Audubon. When John was very young, his mother died. His father remarried and took him and his younger sister Rosa to Nantes, France, to live with their stepmother, Anne Moynet Audubon. She loved John and Rosa as if they were her own. She told John so often that he was the most handsome boy in all of France that he soon came to believe it. She spoiled him. If John came home to dinner late, with dirt on his sleeves and mud on his shoes, she did not scold him. Instead, she would smile at her lovable stepson with his bright blue eyes and wavy chestnut-colored hair and tell the cook to warm up his dinner. John's father was not so easy to please.

Captain *Jean Audubon* was a successful merchant who imported cotton, sugar, and coffee from Santo Domingo and America to France. He wanted his son to grow up to be a sea captain, too. He told John to study geography, music, dancing, fencing, and, most important, mechanical drawing and arithmetic. John was good at some of those subjects. He danced easily and naturally. Fencing was fun for him, too, and using the sword correctly was almost like doing gymnastics. He liked music, and he played the violin, flute, and flageolet, an instrument similar to a penny whistle. He did not like to practice regularly, though. He preferred to take his flageolet to the woods, where he answered the bird calls that were the most beautiful music to his ears. But John hated mechanical drawing and arithmetic! He was terrible in these subjects, and he did everything he could to avoid them. However, if he was to become a sea captain like his father, he would have to be excellent at drawing and arithmetic in order to navigate and keep track of goods on board ship. John's father loved him and worried about his future. He knew his son would not be successful if he failed to study. He warned John that he must spend more time in his room discovering how to multiply and divide and less time in the woods discovering nature's secrets.

Before long, the French Revolution (1789–1799) made it dangerous for John to walk in the woods. Fighting in Nantes made normal life there impossible for the Audubons. The family left the city to live in a farmhouse in Coueron, 5 miles (8 kilometers) down the Loire River.

The Coueron countryside was the most inviting world John had ever known. He spent his days in the woods, looking for birds, bugs, feathers, rocks, and animals. John's stepmother did not force him to do anything he did not want to do. So when Captain Audubon was gone, John forgot about his

As a young boy, Audubon lived in this farmhouse in Coueron, France, where he loved to roam in the woods.

arithmetic and most of his other studies and spent his time as he pleased.

One day, Captain Audubon returned home after a long ocean voyage. He wanted to see how much his children had learned while he was away. Rosa proudly played a new piece on the piano. Pleased by his daughter's progress, the captain gave her a book as a present. Then he turned to his son, now fourteen years old. John gulped and hung his head. He took his violin out of its case, and there for all to see was a very neglected instrument. It was missing some strings and had not been played in a month. Then the captain told John to show him his latest mechanical drawings. All John could find in his cluttered bedroom were a few messy sketches. When his father asked him to do some arithmetic problems, John got them all wrong. It was clear he had not been studying. Captain Audubon was a man of few words, but he made quick decisions.

At dawn the next morning, the captain awakened John. He told him to pack a trunk full of clothes, get his violin, and say good-bye to his stepmother. Then the captain and John climbed into a waiting carriage. Mrs. Audubon tried to hold back her tears as the driver flicked the reins and the carriage pulled away. The captain said nothing. He just opened a book and began reading. John knew better than to interrupt him by asking questions. Nervously, he wondered where they were going.

The journey ended at a military academy at the naval base of Rochefort. Captain Audubon was determined that his son would finally learn some discipline. He intended for John's experience at Rochefort to turn him into a responsible young man. It did not work out that way.

John hated everything about the naval training school. The teachers were strict, and the work was boring. One day, when he was given especially hard arithmetic problems to do, John watched his teacher closely. When the teacher was not paying attention, John jumped out the window! He escaped to the forest—but not for long. A corporal quickly found John and kept him under close guard until his father returned.

Sighing with disappointment, the captain gave up trying to turn his son into a sailor. He sent John back to Coueron.

What was to become of this boy who was not interested in the best education money could buy, who wanted only to roam the woods?

The next time the captain was in Coueron, John showed him his collection of "treasures" gathered from the forest. With pride, he held out nests, dead (and smelly) birds, dried leaves, and bright feathers. When his father expressed an interest in his beloved birds, John brought out some drawings he had done of them. The pictures were far from perfect, and John knew it. He told his father that he often crumpled them up and began again, and again. The captain looked at his son with amazement. At last, here was something that John *did* work at! Wanting to give his son every opportunity he could, Captain Audubon decided to send John to Paris to study art with the most famous painter of the time, Jacques-Louis David. Off to Paris John went, eager to learn how to paint pictures of colorful birds that would look as real as they did singing on a tree branch in the forest.

But to John's disappointment, David's strict lessons focused on drawing black-and-white pictures

Audubon was sent to Paris to study with Jacques-Louis David, shown here in a self-portrait. But he felt trapped in the famous painter's studio.

of huge sculptures of people's heads. There was no mention of animals of any kind, and certainly not birds. John felt trapped in David's studio. He had no interest in drawing the heads of statues. He knew what he wanted to do—draw the most beautiful of the world's creatures. He returned home to Coueron.

In 1803, *Captain Audubon* worried more than usual about his son. General Napoleon Bonaparte was looking for young men to draft into his army. Captain Audubon had fought in battles, and he did not want John to face the same dangers.

In the fall of 1803, Captain Audubon had a plan for his eighteen-year-old son to leave home once again—this time for America. John's heart was pounding with excitement. He barely listened to his father's serious words about learning English and becoming more responsible. He was going to board a ship bound for the most wild and wonderful place in the world!

After a long ocean voyage, John arrived in New York. The woods of the New World seemed to him like a marvelous present he could not wait to open. He soon learned to speak English and before long moved to Mill Grove, a 200-acre (81-hectare) farm in Pennsylvania. Captain Audubon had bought it years before as an investment. It was managed by William Thomas and his wife.

John loved everything about Mill Grove. The farmhouse sat on top of a hill, granting a beautiful view of the green valley below. Perkiomen Creek ran through the property. Rows of hemlock trees, steep bluffs, and big boulders added to the wild feeling of the place. John did what he liked best— hunting, fishing, drawing, and playing his violin. He bought excellent horses and rode them through the woods. And for the pleasure of it, he painted the birds he saw.

When a new family moved into a big house a quarter of a mile from Mill Grove, John paid little attention. Mrs. Thomas suggested that John walk over and welcome them. But he was too busy getting to know the creatures of the forests to worry about getting to know his human neighbors.

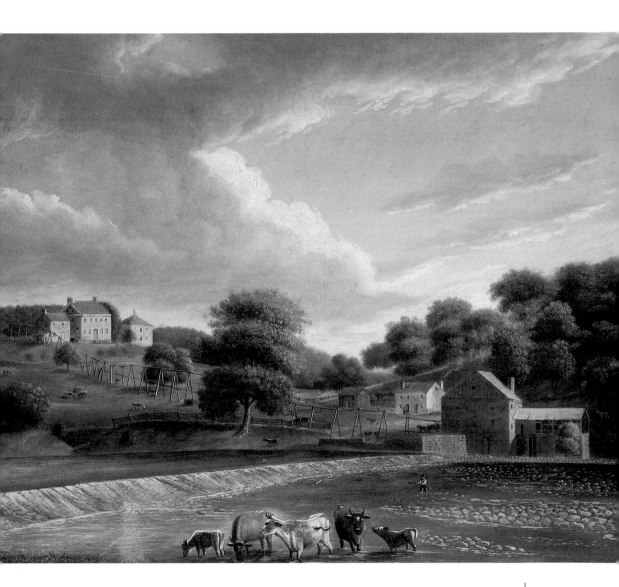

Audubon's first home in the United States was Mill Grove, a farm in Pennsylvania.

15

Hiking in the woods one day, John met an older man who loved nature as much as he did. They talked about birds, hunting, dogs, and horses. They had a lot in common. To John's surprise, it turned out that this man was his new neighbor. His name was William Bakewell. Mr. Bakewell invited John to visit his home, where he met his oldest daughter, Lucy. He liked Lucy right away, and she was charmed by handsome John.

John became good friends not only with Lucy, but also with her brother Thomas. One winter day, John, Thomas, and several other young men went hunting. What fun they had! Perkiomen Creek was frozen hard, so they skated across its icy surface. When darkness fell, they realized they should head home. John took the lead, laughing and holding up a stick with a white kerchief tied to it so that the others could see to follow him. He skated faster and faster, the cold air making his rosy cheeks tingle. Suddenly he saw a hole in the ice right in front of him. He tried to skid his skates to a stop, but it was too late.

John fell into the cold creek, and the current quickly pulled him down. His friends could not see where he had been swept. They yelled and cried out for him, but he was trapped under the ice.

John was very lucky. At another hole in the ice farther downstream, he managed to pull himself out of the creek. Trembling from the cold, he crawled onto solid ice. What a relief! The young men knew they had almost lost their good-natured, fun-loving friend. They did not know that the world had nearly lost one of its greatest nature artists!

One afternoon at Mill Grove, John noticed a small nest fastened to a rocky ledge not far from Perkiomen Creek. He climbed up to get a good look and discovered that it was near the entrance to a cave. Curious, he went inside. That spot became his favorite hideaway—the perfect place to draw birds, read, or just sit and think. In the spring, he watched a pair of phoebes build a new nest. When the female laid an egg, John nearly burst for joy. He wrote in his journal, "That sight pleased me more than if I had seen a diamond of the size. In that frail covering life already existed." Soon five more eggs were added to the nest.

*Audubon visited a pair of phoebes so often that
the birds allowed him to pet their babies.*

John studied those birds so much that he neglected a new project on the property. Captain Audubon had hired Francis Dacosta from Nantes, France, to come to the United States to help run Mill Grove. Dacosta, William Thomas, and John decided to reopen a lead mine that had been operated there years before. Dacosta and Thomas busied themselves with the mine, but John was more interested in the phoebes. He visited the cave so often that the birds grew used to him, even allowing him to pet their babies.

John watched the adult phoebes dart from branches to catch flies in midair. With the flies in their beaks, they flew to the nest to feed their young. John wondered: Would those same birds return to his cave the next year? To find out, he tied tiny silver threads to their legs. But the birds bit the threads until they fell off. After several tries, John managed to tie the threads so the birds could not remove them. Next spring, he would see if any phoebes that nested by the cave wore those silver threads. John was probably the first person in the United States to identify individual birds in this way, a method scientists called "bird banding," which was not generally started until one hundred years later!

John loved painting birds, even though he had a problem—binoculars had not been invented yet. Except for the tame phoebes, most birds could be studied only from a distance. John could not see the details, such as a colored pattern on a bird's wing or stripes on its head. He often used his gun to shoot a bird so that he could examine it closely before drawing it. But he was not satisfied with his results. He wanted the birds in his paintings to look alive, but he needed models that stood still. Living birds flew away. How could he solve this problem?

One morning John thought of a way. He jumped out of bed, rode to the woods, and shot the first bird he saw, a kingfisher. Then he used wires to hold it up in a natural-looking position. Instead of painting a dead bird lying flat on a table, he painted the kingfisher in a lifelike pose. It was the best painting he had done up until then.

John loved the birds at Mill Grove, and he grew to love a special person, too. He wanted to marry

*Audubon's pictures, such as this engraving of
a wild turkey, showed birds in lifelike poses.*

Lucy Bakewell. But John's father insisted that before his son got married, he needed to be able to earn his own living. The captain could not support John and a wife, too. His investments in Santo Domingo had failed because of a revolution there, and he was getting old and tired. John had to take responsibility for himself.

The lead mine at Mill Grove was not turning out as well as Dacosta, Thomas, and John had hoped. The operation was losing money. John blamed Dacosta for the failure of the mine, but John himself had spent most of his time studying and painting the birds and had not paid much attention to the business. He had gained a lot of knowledge about birds, but that did not provide an income.

John wanted his father to allow him to marry Lucy, and he also wanted to convince his father that Dacosta was responsible for the failure of the mine. He sailed to France. What a reunion the Audubon family enjoyed on John's surprise arrival! His stepmother said that he was even more handsome than before, and the captain beamed at his son. But Napoleon was still drafting young men into his army, and it would not be safe for John to stay in France long.

Captain Audubon and his wealthy friend Francis Rozier came up with a plan. Rozier's son Ferdinand had just been released from Napoleon's army, and he wanted to leave France. Captain Audubon no longer had much money, but Rozier did. And because of his experience and friends, the captain knew how to arrange a safe ocean voyage. The fathers put their heads together and made arrangements for their sons to sail to America in 1806 on the ship *Polly.*

The trip started off well until an English pirate ship, the *Rattlesnake,* fired on the *Polly.* John rushed to get his money. He wrapped it in some old clothes and hid it under a cable near the front of the ship. The British pirates came on board, kidnapped two of the sailors, and robbed the passengers. They searched for gold but found little. After the *Rattlesnake* sailed out of sight, John ran to the cable. Underneath were his clothes, with his gold coins still hidden inside them.

When he was twenty-one, John Audubon walked to Philadelphia to apply for United States citizenship.

John Audubon married Lucy Bakewell, his neighbor at Mill Grove, on April 8, 1808.

In May 1806, John and his friend landed in New York and then traveled to Mill Grove. John could not have been more pleased by what he found. Lucy still loved him. And some of the phoebes in the cave wore tiny silver threads on their legs!

Ferdinand Rozier turned out to be a good partner for John. Rozier had good business sense, and he worked out an agreement with Dacosta for the handling of the mine and Mill Grove. John spent his time hunting, painting, training his dog, playing his violin, and enjoying Lucy's company.

One day, John walked 24 miles (39 kilometers) to Philadelphia and entered the office of the district court. He applied to become a citizen of the United States. John James Audubon was officially an American.

Captain Audubon and Mr. Bakewell both felt that John and Lucy should not marry until John had enough income to support himself and a wife. To earn money, John worked as a clerk for Lucy's uncle, Benjamin Bakewell, a successful merchant in New York City. But John did not like business, and he did poorly at it.

The next year John and his friend Rozier decided to try something new. But first, John convinced Lucy's father to let them get married. On April 8, 1808, she became his bride. Victor Gifford Audubon, their first son, was born on June 26, 1809.

John and Rozier opened a store in Louisville, Kentucky, then a small city of only a thousand people. Rozier took care of the store most of the time. John did not like working there. He grew bored standing behind the counter, waiting for customers to come in. He preferred traveling to buy things they could sell in the store. He especially liked going through the wild parts of Kentucky, Ohio, and Pennsylvania, because the woods were filled with beautiful birds. John continued to paint, and by 1810 he had more than two hundred life-size pictures of American birds.

One day, when John was working at the store in Louisville, a stranger with a tame parakeet perched on his shoulder walked in. The man introduced himself as Alexander Wilson, and he said

This print shows the Ohio River at Louisville, Kentucky, a few years before Audubon and his partner, Ferdinand Rozier, opened a store there.

Audubon's painting of passenger pigeons. Once plentiful, the birds were hunted so much that they totally died out, or became extinct.

that he was selling paintings he had done of American birds. John was amazed! He had never heard of Wilson before. John was just about to buy the paintings when Rozier took him aside. Speaking in French so that Wilson could not understand him, Rozier said to John, "My dear Audubon, what induces you to subscribe to this work? Your drawings are certainly far better, and you must know as much of the habits of American birds as this gentleman." So John did not buy Wilson's paintings; instead, he showed Wilson what *he* had done. Wilson was impressed, and he asked John if he planned to sell his work. John said no, but he started thinking about what Wilson was trying to do—make money from paintings of birds. Wilson died just a few years later, but John never forgot him.

Rozier and John tried running a store in Henderson, 125 miles (200 kilometers) down the Ohio River. They did not do well there either. John was not cut out to be a businessman. At a moment's notice he would leave his store to go hunting with Indians or scouting the woods to find a bird singing a melody he had not heard before. Very patient with his unreliable business partner, Rozier suggested they open a store in Ste. Genevieve, on the Mississippi River. John advised Lucy to wait in Henderson. He wanted to find out what Ste. Genevieve was like before his family joined him.

The trip to Ste. Genevieve was filled with adventure. Ice clogged the river, so John and Rozier had to wait for it to clear. Rozier was impatient to be on his way, but John loved the wilds of the Mississippi. They built a log cabin for shelter while they waited out the winter weather. John made friends with the Indians, who appreciated a portrait he drew of one of them. Every day John hunted and drew pictures of wild turkey, bears, cougars, and raccoons.

When the ice melted, John and Rozier continued their trip. But when John got to Ste. Genevieve, he did not like it. He sold his share of the business to Rozier and hurried back to Henderson to be with his family.

John and Lucy had another son, John Woodhouse Audubon, in 1812. They later had two daughters; both died when they were only babies. John set up a mill in Henderson, but it lost money. John and Lucy were poor, but they had one very impor-

Audubon's pictures of animals, such as these mountain lions, were based on his travels in the wilderness.

*Like the passenger pigeon, the whooping crane
was common when Audubon painted this picture.
Today the birds are very rare.*

tant thing—love. John later wrote of Lucy, "With her, was not I always rich?"

n 1820, John came up with what he called his "great idea." He decided he would find a way to publish his drawings. The book would be a collection of all the American birds, shown in natural settings. He had painted the pictures the same size as the birds themselves, and he wanted the published pictures to be life-size, too. For a year he traveled the southern states to find new birds to paint. Lucy supported John's idea, even though he had to be away from her and the children.

John collected and painted many kinds of birds, and he kept a journal with notes about their habits. He worked tirelessly. For John, the project was a passion. But to make his great idea a reality, he needed a publisher. Unable to find one in America, John decided to try his luck in England. It would take them years to earn enough money to pay for the expensive trip. He made some money painting pictures of people, and Lucy worked as a teacher in Louisiana. By 1826 they had saved enough.

In England, John made friends easily. He was handsome and likable. His talents as an artist and naturalist were quickly recognized. People were amazed at how alive the birds in his paintings looked. Each seemed to have its own personality. Within ten days of his arrival, his artwork was exhibited at the Royal Institution in Liverpool.

John loved to tell stories. He fascinated listeners in Europe with his descriptions of the forests and birds of the New World. He became known as "the American Woodsman."

In Edinburgh, Scotland, he met William Lizars, a printer and engraver. Lizars said he would publish John's paintings. His great idea was about to become a reality!

But problems arose. Publishing four hundred large illustrations in one book was out of the question because of the expense. So the plan was to print the book in eighty sections, with five pictures (or "plates") in each. John needed to sell subscriptions to the book, in the same way that magazine subscriptions are sold now. Each subscriber would receive one section five times a year. In February 1827, Lizars printed the first plates. Showing them

These items belonged to the "American Woodsman," as Audubon was known in Europe: his hat, buffalo-skin case made by Mandan Indians, double-barreled shotgun, pistol, and Mandan war club.

as examples, John set off to find wealthy subscribers so that production could continue. He needed to use all his charm to finance *Birds of America.* John had never been good at business, but he was determined to succeed this time; after all, *Birds of America* depended on it! Then William Lizars's workers went on strike. The project came to a halt. John was filled with despair until he met Robert Havell, a young engraver in London. Havell offered to publish the book if John could get enough subscribers.

For three years John traveled around Europe looking for subscribers. He did paintings and oil portraits to support himself, but his main concern was financing *Birds of America.* And he succeeded!

9ohn missed Lucy very much. He returned to America in 1829 to join her in Louisiana. Together they traveled to Louisville to visit their sons, who were now young men. By this time John was famous. In fact, President Andrew Jackson invited John and Lucy to have dinner with him at the White House in Washington, D.C. American statesman Edward Everett arranged for Audubon's work to be shown

The engraver Robert Havell offered to publish Birds of America *if Audubon could get enough subscribers.*

Engraving of the prints was completed in Havell's London shop in 1838.

to members of Congress, and for the Library of Congress to subscribe to *Birds of America.*

In the spring of 1830, John and Lucy sailed to Europe. In Edinburgh, John began writing a book about the birds he had drawn. He wrote from four o'clock in the morning until ten or eleven o'clock at night. The first volume of his *Ornithological Biography* was published in 1831 (*ornithological* means "having to do with birds"). Meanwhile, *Birds of America* was being published according to schedule.

John and Lucy returned to America, and their son Victor went to England to oversee the continuing publication of *Birds of America.* Victor had a good head for business. John's other son was an artist like his father. They traveled together, collecting and drawing more birds.

Birds of America was completed in 1838. Then John published a smaller, less expensive edition of the book. It became a best-seller.

John and Lucy did not need to worry about money anymore. They bought land in Carmansville, which is now part of New York City. From the porch of their house, they could sit and watch the

After the success of Birds of America, *Audubon moved to this home on the Hudson River, in New York.*

As the famous naturalist grew older, his hair turned white and he wore a long, flowing beard.

Hudson River below and hear the birds singing in the orchard.

John did not need to work, but he did anyway, because his love of painting continued. He turned his attention to American animals. Again he worked fourteen hours a day. His sons helped him, and publication began of *The Vivaparous Quadrupeds of North America* ("vivaparous quadrupeds" are four-legged animals that do not lay eggs, such as rabbits, bears, and mice). In 1843 he traveled the Missouri River to find more animals to paint. At the end of the year he returned home, bringing with him many new specimens. To preserve the animals, he put them in barrels of rum!

As John got older, his age began to show. His hair turned white, and he had a long, flowing beard. His eyesight grew poor. It broke his heart when he could no longer see well enough to draw. He wrote, "I am growing old fast." He died on January 27, 1851, at the age of sixty-six.

After John's death, Lucy started a school for children who lived nearby. One of her young pupils was George Grinnell. He grew up to become a lover of birds, and he founded an organization whose goal is to protect them. He named it the Audubon Society. Today more than half a million Americans belong to the National Audubon Society. Like John, they love the woods and the birds that live in them.

Important Dates

April 26, 1785   John James Audubon is born in
                      Santo Domingo.

1789   Captain Audubon brings John and
                      Rosa to live in Nantes, France, with
                      their stepmother Anne Moynet
                      Audubon.

1800   John attends naval training school
                      at Rochefort.

1802   John studies (briefly) with painter
                      Jacques-Louis David in Paris.

1803   John sails to America.

1804	John settles at Mill Grove, his father's farm in Pennsylvania.
April 8, 1808	John marries Lucy Bakewell.
June 26, 1809	Victor Gifford Audubon is born.
November 30, 1812	John Woodhouse Audubon is born.
1819	After John failed many times as a store owner, his mill in Henderson, Kentucky, goes bankrupt.
1820	John comes up with his "great idea": to publish a collection of all his life-size paintings of American birds.
1826–1829	John travels to Europe to find a publisher for *Birds of America* and people to subscribe to it.
1831	The first volume of the *Ornithological Biography* is published.
1838	The final plates of *Birds of America* are completed.
1839	The best-selling smaller edition of *Birds of America* is published.
1843	John travels the Missouri River to collect more animals to paint for *The Vivaparous Quadrupeds of North America.*
January 27, 1851	John dies at the age of sixty-six.

Further Reading

Audubon and His Sons. Amy Hogeboom (Lothrop, Lee & Shepard, 1956).

Audubon's Birds of America: The Audubon Society Baby Elephant Folio. Roger Tory Peterson and Virginia Marie Peterson (Abbeville Press, 1981).

John Audubon, Boy Naturalist. Miriam E. Mason (Bobbs-Merrill, 1962).

John James Audubon. Margaret and John Kieran (Random House, 1954).

A Kid's First Book of Birdwatching. Scott Weidensaul (Running Press, 1990).

Index